First Facts®

easy origami

EASY HOLIDAY
Origami

by Christopher L. Harbo

CAPSTONE PRESS
a capstone imprint

First Facts is published by Capstone Press,
151 Good Counsel Drive, P.O. Box 669, Mankato, Minnesota 56002.
www.capstonepub.com

 Books published by Capstone Press are manufactured with paper containing at least 10 percent post-consumer waste.

Library of Congress Cataloging-in-Publication Data
Harbo, Christopher L.
  Easy holiday origami / by Christopher L. Harbo.
    p. cm.—(First facts. Easy origami)
  Includes bibliographical references.
  Summary: "Provides instructions and photo-illustrated diagrams for making a variety of easy holiday
origami models"—Provided by publisher.
  ISBN 978-1-4296-5387-9 (library binding)
  1. Origam—Juvenile literature. 2. Holiday decorations—Juvenile literature. I. Title. II. Series.

TT870.H32 2011
736'.982—dc22   2010024785

Editorial Credits
Designer: ALISON THIELE
Photo Studio Specialist: SARAH SCHUETTE
Scheduler: MARCY MORIN
Production Specialist: LAURA MANTHE

Photo Credits
Capstone Studio/Karon Dubke, all photos

Artistic Effects
Shutterstock/F. Veronica, jihane, Kar, Mackey Creations, Oksana Merzlyakova,
    Sarah Angeltun, Sergey Lazarev, TatjanaRittner, Volkova Anna

ABOUT THE AUTHOR

Christopher L. Harbo loves origami. He began folding paper several years ago and hasn't quit since. In addition to decorative origami, he also enjoys folding paper airplanes. When he's not practicing origami, Christopher spends his free time reading Japanese comic books and watching movies.

Printed in the United States of America in North Mankato, Minnesota.
092010   005933CGS11

TABLE OF Contents

HOLIDAY Smiles

Celebrate holidays throughout the year with origami. Warm someone's heart on Valentine's Day with a pocket heart. Honor your country on the Fourth of July with a five-point star. Fold a silverware server to dress up a dinner table on Thanksgiving. The seven models in this book are easy to fold and a blast to share. Give the gift of origami. You're sure to make people smile.

MATERIALS

Origami is a simple art that doesn't use many materials. You'll only need the following things to complete the projects in this book:

Ruler: Some models use measurements to complete. A ruler will help you measure.

Origami Paper: Square origami paper comes in many fun colors and sizes. You can buy this paper in most craft stores.

Letter-sized Paper: Not all origami models begin with a square. Use 8.5- by 11-inch (22- by 28-centimeter) paper when needed.

Pencil: Use a pencil when you need to mark spots you measure with the ruler.

Clear Tape: Most origami models don't need tape. But when they do, you'll be glad you have it handy.

Scissors: Sometimes a model needs a snip here or there to complete. Keep a scissors nearby.

FOLDING TECHNIQUES

Folding paper is easier when you understand basic origami folds and symbols. Practice the folds on this list before trying the models in this book. Turn back to this list if you get stuck on a tricky step, or ask an adult for help.

Valley Folds are represented by a dashed line. One side of the paper is folded against the other like a book. A sharp fold is made by running your finger along the fold line.

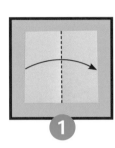

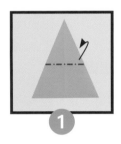

Mountain Folds are represented by a pink or white dashed and dotted line. The paper is folded sharply behind the model.

Squash Folds are formed by lifting one edge of a pocket. The pocket gets folded again so the spine gets flattened. The existing fold lines become new edges.

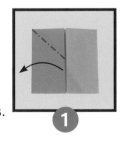

Inside reverse folds are made by opening a pocket slightly. Then you fold the model inside itself along existing fold lines.

Outside reverse folds are made by opening a pocket slightly. Then you fold the model outside itself along existing fold lines.

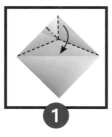

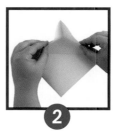

Rabbit ear folds are formed by bringing two edges of a point together using existing fold lines. The new point is folded to one side.

SYMBOLS

SINGLE-POINTED ARROW: Fold the paper in the direction of the arrow.

HALF-POINTED ARROW: Fold the paper behind.

DOUBLE-POINTED ARROW: Fold the paper and then unfold it.

LOOPING ARROW: Turn the paper over or turn it to a new position.

SILVERWARE Server

Traditional Model

A great Thanksgiving dinner starts with a well-set table. Give your silverware some style with this simple server.

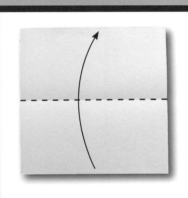

1

Start with the colored side of the paper face down. Valley fold the bottom edge to the top edge.

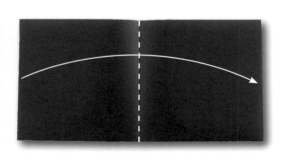

2

Valley fold the left edge to the right edge. You now have four layers of paper.

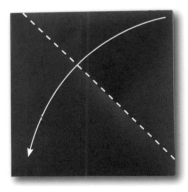

3

Valley fold the point of the top layer. This point should rest about .5 inch (1.3 cm) from the bottom point of the paper.

4

Valley fold the point of the second layer. This point should rest about 1 inch (2.5 cm) from the bottom point of the paper.

5

Valley fold the point of the third layer. This point should rest about 1.5 inches (3.8 cm) from the bottom point of the paper.

6

Mountain fold the corners of the model. Allow them to overlap slightly in back.

7

The model will now hold silverware. Tuck it snuggly into the pocket.

8

Your silverware server is ready for the table.

 **SECRET Tip** Use a 12-inch (30.5-cm) square or larger for this model. A large square napkin also works well.

POCKET Heart

Designed by Christopher L. Harbo

Surprise someone special with a pocket heart on Valentine's Day. This clever model can hold secret messages or a handful of candy.

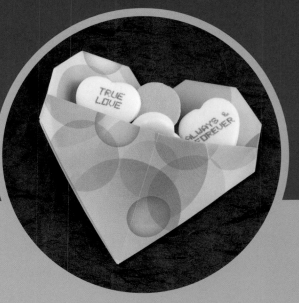

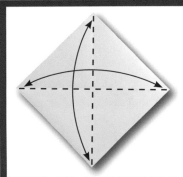

1

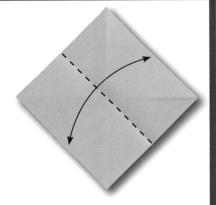

Start with the colored side of the paper face down. Valley fold the left point to the right point and unfold. Valley fold the bottom point to the top point and unfold.

2

Turn the paper over.

Valley fold the bottom-left edge to the top-right edge. Then unfold the paper.

3

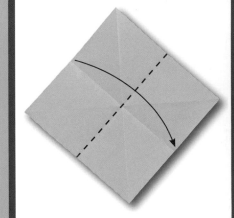

Valley fold the top-left edge to bottom-right edge.

4

5

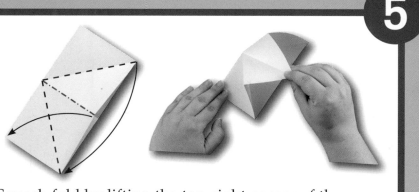

Squash fold by lifting the top-right corner of the paper. Push the corner down and to the left on the existing folds. Flatten the paper into a diamond shape.

6

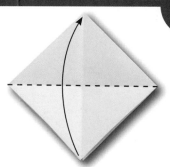

Valley fold the top layer's bottom point so it meets the top point. Repeat this step on the back of the model.

7

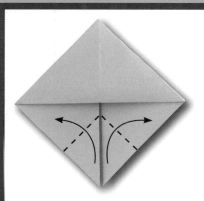

Valley fold the bottom points so they rest along the edges. Leave a .25-inch (.64-cm) gap between the triangles you make and the center edge of the model.

8

Valley fold the two bottom points. Then valley fold the two side points.

9

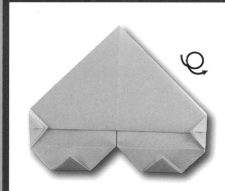

Turn the model over. Then turn the model halfway around so the heart is upright.

10

Fill the pocket heart with candy for your Valentine.

SECRET Tip

Tape the folded corners on the back of the model to make the pocket stronger.

FIVE-POINT Star

Traditional Model

Stories say Betsy Ross made these stars for the first United States flag. Now you can make Fourth of July stars with one snip of a scissors.

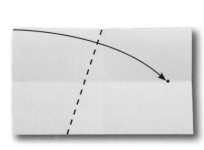

1

Cut a 1-inch (2.5-cm) strip off the top of a letter-sized sheet of paper. Recycle the thin strip, but keep the larger piece of paper.

2

Valley fold the top edge to the bottom edge.

3

Valley fold the left edge to the right edge and unfold. Valley fold the bottom edge to the top edge and unfold.

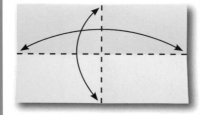

Valley fold the top-left corner to the long fold line running across the paper. Note how the valley fold meets the fold running down the paper.

4

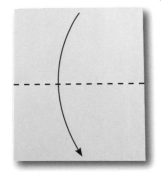

5

Valley fold the right corner to the left edge.

6

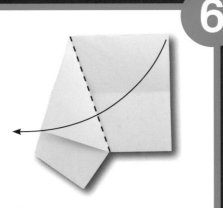

Valley fold the top-right corner along the fold from step 5.

7

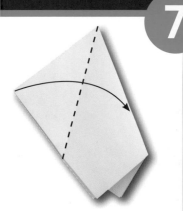

Valley fold the left corner to the right edge.

8

Use a ruler and a pencil to mark the left edge of the model. The mark should be about 1.5 inches (3.8 cm) from the top point.

9

Note how the top layer of paper forms a triangle. Cut the paper from the corner of this triangle to the pencil mark from step 8.

10

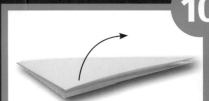

Unfold the small triangle you snipped off in step 9.

11

Ta-da! You have a perfect five-point star!

SECRET Tip Make smaller stars with 4.25- by 5-inch (10.8- by 12.7-cm) pieces of paper. In step 8, make your mark 1 inch (2.5 cm) from the top point.

13

Tulip AND Stem

Traditional Model

How do you celebrate the first day of May? These paper tulips will brighten any May Day basket.

TULIP

1

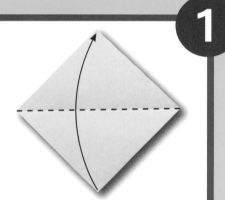

Start with the colored side of the paper face down. Valley fold the bottom point to the top point.

2

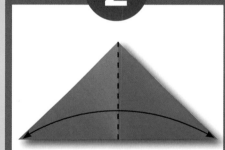

Valley fold the left point to the right point and unfold.

3

Valley fold the left and right points up. Allow them to rest slightly to the left and right of the center fold.

4

Mountain fold the left and right corners behind the model.

5

Your tulip blossom is ready for a stem.

14

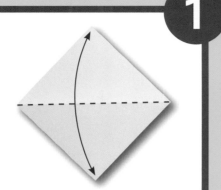
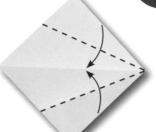
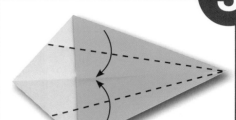

1

Start with the colored side of the paper face down. Valley fold the top point to the bottom point and unfold.

2

Valley fold the top-right edge to the center fold. Valley fold the bottom-right edge to the center fold.

3

Valley fold the top-right edge to the center fold. Valley fold the bottom-right edge to the center fold.

4

Valley fold the top-left edge to the center fold. Valley fold the bottom-left edge to the center fold.

5

Valley fold the left point to the right side. Allow the left point to rest about 2 inches (5 cm) from the right point.

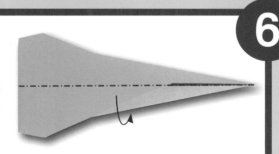

6

Mountain fold the bottom half of the model behind the top half.

7

Your finished stem is ready for a flower. Attached the stem to the back of the tulip with a small piece of tape.

SECRET TIP Pull the stem's leaf out slightly to make your flower more lifelike.

LEPRECHAUN'S Cap

Traditional Model

You don't have to be Irish to enjoy St. Patrick's Day. Find your inner leprechaun by wearing this festive cap.

1

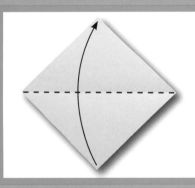

Start with the colored side of the paper face down. Valley fold the bottom point to the top point.

2

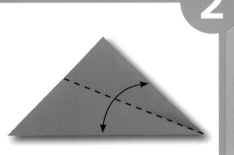

Valley fold the paper's top layer so the right edge meets the bottom edge. Make a crisp fold and then unfold.

3

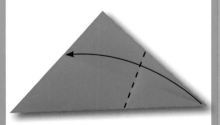

Valley fold the right point to the left edge. The point should rest on the fold from step 2.

4

Valley fold the left point to the right corner.

16

5

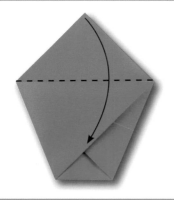

Valley fold the top layer's point down. The fold should run along the edges formed in steps 3 and 4. Repeat this step on the back side of the model.

6

Turn the model halfway around so it is upside down.

7

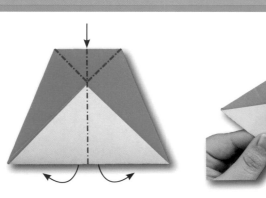

Open the bottom of the model while pressing down on the top. Flatten the model completely.

8

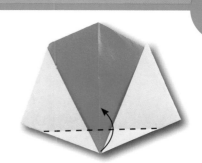

Valley fold the top layer of the bottom edge. Repeat this step on the back side of the model.

9

Pull out the left and right flaps. Flatten the model to hold the flaps in place.

10

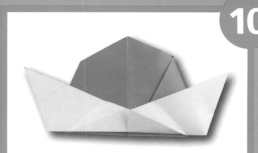

Put on your leprechaun's cap, and hunt for a pot of gold!

SECRET Tip

Use a 22-inch (56-cm) square of newspaper to make a cap large enough to wear.

MINIATURE Scrapbook

Traditional Model

A tiny book of memories makes a great gift for Mother's Day or Father's Day. Fold a miniature scrapbook, and fill it with photos, drawings, and stories.

1

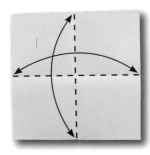

Start with the colored side of the paper face down. Valley fold the left edge to the right edge and unfold. Valley fold the bottom edge to the top edge and unfold.

2

Valley fold the top edge to the center fold.

3

Turn the paper over.

4

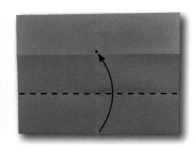

Valley fold the bottom edge so that it rests just past the center fold.

5

Valley fold the left and right edges to the center fold.

6

Valley fold the inside corners of the top layers to the left and right edges.

7

Pull out the left and right sides. Tuck the folds made in step 6 behind the model.

8

Use a scissors to cut along the left and right edges. Also cut along the center fold. These cuts should extend to the middle of the model.

9

Mountain fold the bottom half of the model to the back and unfold.

10

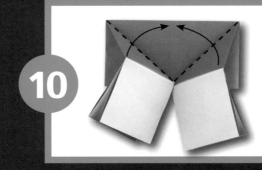

Valley fold the left and right sides to the top edge. The folds you made in step 9 will allow your pages to swing toward the center.

11

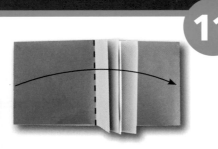

Valley fold the left edge to the right edge.

12

Fill your finished miniature scrapbook with memories!

 **SECRET Tip** Use a 10-inch (25-cm) square to make a miniature scrapbook. This book will fit well inside a pocket or a purse.

HOLIDAY Stocking

Traditional Model adapted by Rick Beech

Be Santa's helper with this holiday stocking. Stuff it with tiny treasures such as chocolates and peppermint sticks.

1

Start with the colored side of the paper face up. Valley fold a .25-inch (.64-cm) wide strip at the top of the paper.

2

Turn the paper over.

3

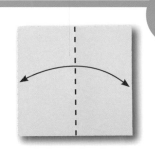

Valley fold the left edge to the right edge and unfold.

4

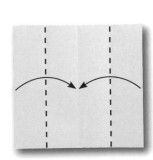

Valley fold the left and right edges to the center fold.

5

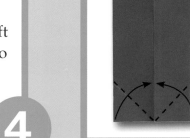

Valley fold the bottom-left corner to the center fold. Valley fold the bottom-right corner to the center fold.

6

Valley fold the bottom point to the edge from step 5.

7

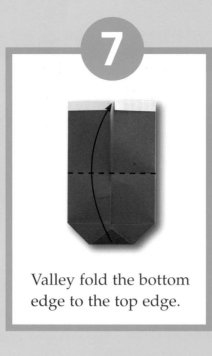

Valley fold the bottom edge to the top edge.

8

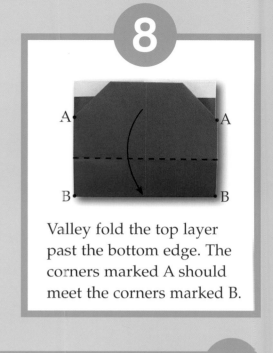

Valley fold the top layer past the bottom edge. The corners marked A should meet the corners marked B.

9

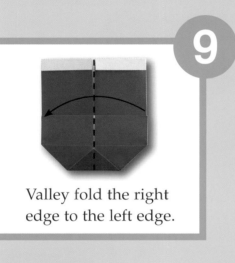

Valley fold the right edge to the left edge.

10

Pinch the left edge of the model with your left hand. Pinch the model's toe with your right hand. Gently pull the toe down and to the right to move it outward. Then flatten the model to hold the new folds in place.

11

Open the back of the model. Tuck the top flap's border under the back flap's border. The top of the stocking now has a pocket.

12

Fill your holiday stocking with goodies, just like Santa!

SECRET Tip The holiday stocking makes a great gift tag on Christmas presents.

Origami
ALL YEAR LONG

MAY

DECEMBER

MARCH

JUNE

NOVEMBER

JULY

FEBRUARY

READ More

Boonyadhistarn, Thiranut. *Origami: The Fun and Funky Art of Paper Folding.* Crafts. Mankato, Minn.: Capstone Press, 2007.

Boursin, Didier. *Folding for Fun.* Richmond Hill, Ont.: Firefly Books, 2007.

Engel, Peter. *10-Fold Origami: Fabulous Paperfolds You Can Make in 10 Steps or Less.* New York: Sterling Pub. Co., Inc., 2008.

Meinking, Mary. *Easy Origami.* Origami. Mankato, Minn.: Capstone Press, 2009.

Shingu, Fumiaki. *Easy Origami.* New York: Mud Puddle Books, 2007.

INTERNET Sites

FactHound offers a safe, fun way to find Internet sites related to this book. All of the sites on FactHound have been researched by our staff.

Here's all you do:

Visit *www.facthound.com*

Type in this code: 9781429653879

Check out projects, games and lots more at
www.capstonekids.com